From Goo to God

A Science-Based Defense of Creationism vs. Evolution

"Always be prepared to give an answer to everyone who asks you to give the reason for the hope that you have. But do this with gentleness and respect" (1 Peter 3:15).

Bruce R. Matson

Library of Congress Control Number: 2020908214
ISBN-13:   Paperback: 978-1-64749-111-6
            ePub: 978-1-64749-112-3

Printed in the United States of America

GoToPublish LLC
1-888-337-1724
www.gotopublish.com
info@gotopublish.com

Dedication

I dedicate this book to my parents, Roger and Marilyn. They have always supported and encouraged me through the many ups and downs of my life. When times were tough, I always knew my loving parents would be there for me and love me unconditionally. My parents always taught me to treat people with dignity and respect and to honor our good name and faith. I love them very much, and, therefore, dedicate this book in their honor.

Contents

Preface

The purpose of this book is two-fold, both of which are equally important. First of all, I hope to give fellow believers in Christ tools, in the form of scientifically proven facts about the natural world, to support their belief in a Creator and His creation.

"For since the creation of the world God's invisible qualities—his eternal power and divine nature—have been clearly seen, being understood from what has been made, so that people are without excuse" (Romans 1:20).

Secondly, armed with these tools, I want these believers to confidently defend and share their faith with non-believers. My greatest hope and mission is to strengthen current believers, encourage evangelism, and to bring as many non-believers to Christ as possible.

"Opponents must be gently instructed, in the hope that God will grant them repentance leading them to a knowledge of the truth" (2 Timothy 2:25).

Introduction

My name is Bruce Matson and I am an educator of 28 years. Throughout my experiences, at various times, I have taught all subjects from kindergarten through eighth grade. I have also been a school administrator, bus driver, and a coach of football, basketball, and track.

I have seen time and time again in K-12 textbooks the promotion of evolution as fact and ignoring to even mention creationism as an alternative. If creationism is mentioned, it's often in a very short, token blurb, but it's never given any credibility or fair-minded coverage. We see all around us on the TV, at the movies, within video games, and so on, the assumption of evolution as truth. I believe evolutionists have nothing to stand on, so they bombard our society, and especially our kids, with this indoctrination. Unfortunately, many well-meaning people, including Christians, get caught up in it all because they haven't heard the counter argument. Well, that ends now.

Evolution is built on a foundation of sand, and it's time to let the flood waters run. In this book, I share fact after fact that pound away like waves at evolution's shoreline. We who believe in a Creator need to stand firm and challenge the false premises of evolution. As you will see in my book, evolutionists don't have science based facts to stand on, but we do. All they have are theories and assumptions that cannot be proven using the scientific method. Creationists need to finally understand the science is on our side.

This book was written to provide you the tools you need to strengthen your faith and to defend your belief in a Creator. I'm sure that much of this science-based evidence of creation will be new to you, so don't feel bad if you had some uncertainty. But once you are armed with the truth, you can send some waves toward evolution's shoreline yourself. It will crumble.

The evidence in support of creationism is mounting with new scientific discoveries and advances. Creationists no longer need to fear science, but need to embrace it and the evidence it provides. Since God created the universe, true science will always lead us back to the Creator. It's time for creationists to take a public stand and demand the truth to be told, especially in our schools. Our kids deserve better, so speak out and let your voices be heard.

Writing this book is a public profession of my faith in Christ as my Lord and Savior. I hope if you are also a Christian that the facts in this book will give you the confidence to share and defend your faith too. If you are not a believer, I hope you will at least be open-minded enough to think about the facts in this book. That's all I can ask, then your heart, and Christ, will do the rest. "Then you will know the truth, and the truth will set you free" (John 8:32).

Get into the "Goo"

Evolutionists believe that millions of years ago, the first living single-celled organism came into being. They believe that the conditions of temperature, water, inorganic matter, and energy came together in the perfect, necessary way, to spontaneously generate the first living cell. These conditions, in a "just by chance" convergence, happened in the oceans millions of years ago in what some like to call the primordial ooze or "goo".

So let's take a look at the "goo" scientifically. In the history of recorded science, no such claim of "spontaneous generation" has ever been documented or duplicated using the scientific method. Even in the most ideal laboratory conditions of today, no scientist has ever made a living cell or any kind of living matter from inorganic materials. Biogenesis (the teaching that life can only come from life), is a documentable, observable, and repeatable scientific truth.

At best, in 1953, Stanley Miller created several amino acids in a laboratory by simulating Earth's early atmospheric conditions and adding an electric current. This was an attempt to demonstrate "abiogenesis," the claim that life can come from non-living, inorganic compounds. But scientists today know that those amino acids were much simpler than the ones found in the protein molecules of all animals, and of course, they were not living. Even more significantly, the amino acids were not "left-handed," which is a requirement for all living creatures from the most basic one-celled organisms to humans. (Institute for Creation Research)

Recent attempts to replicate and/or improve Miller's process have likewise failed. This is due to the complexity of the protein molecules found in even simple one-celled organisms. And once again, all the amino acids used to construct these proteins must be "left-handed." The odds against these complex "left-handed" sequences randomly occurring in nature are one in 10^{125}. Yes, that's a ten with 125 zeros after it. (Strobel, p. 983) Now, that's overwhelming odds to overcome. Plus, making simplistic amino acids is a long-ways off from producing a living cell.

In the diagrams below, you can see some of the configurations that are necessary structures for carrying out the life processes. But how did the first one-celled organism spontaneously have all the features necessary to protect, move, take in and store energy, use energy, take in necessary nutrients and water, block out harmful substances, and release waste products? What are the odds that all this would perfectly come together by chance?

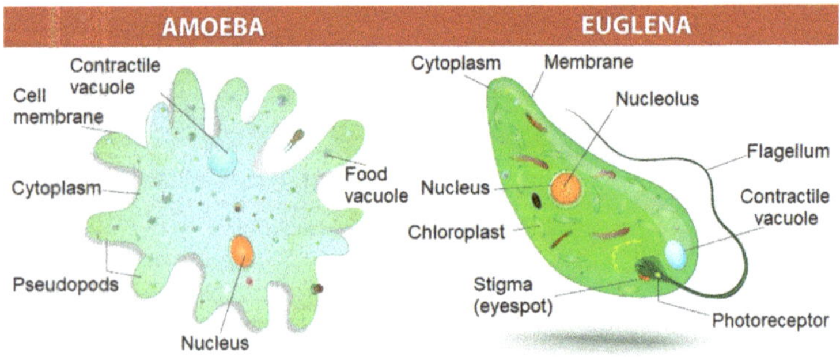

Figure 1

In addition, the fossil record shows that the simplest one-celled organisms of today are very similar in structure to the earliest one-celled organisms ever found. Why aren't the one-celled organisms of today more advanced in structure as evolutionists should expect?

For the sake of argument, let's concede that all these structures and processes did spontaneously come about with this first one-celled organism. But how did it grow? How did it know how to move? How did it know how to eat or to make its own food? And finally, how did it instantly know how to carry out all of the life processes?

An even more confounding question for evolutionists is, *How did it reproduce itself?* Even in one-celled organisms, reproduction is a complex process. So how did this first spontaneous one-celled organism know how to reproduce itself to perpetuate its existence?

Interestingly, simple one-celled organisms have millions of molecules, which are arranged perfectly into individual organs that function together as a cohesive system. This poses another problem for evolutionists to overcome called "irreducible complexity." This means every necessary structure for the life processes must be in place for an organism to function and survive. If even one structure is missing in the system, the organism can't survive. Evolution is, therefore, impossible because the system would be built piece by piece over millions of years, and the system has to be fully present to function. (Strobel, p. 756)

So can any objective person believe the first living cell came to be from non-living, inorganic materials in a random, spontaneous moment?

"Goo" Find the Answers

To address some of the previous questions, one can study the structure and functionality of one-celled organisms today. These organisms are actually quite complex. Some surround and absorb food while others manufacture food through photosynthesis. Some have cilia that propel it around like oars while others have a propeller called a flagellum. How do these one-celled organisms know how to do all of this? Well, thanks to modern day science, we know it's in their DNA.

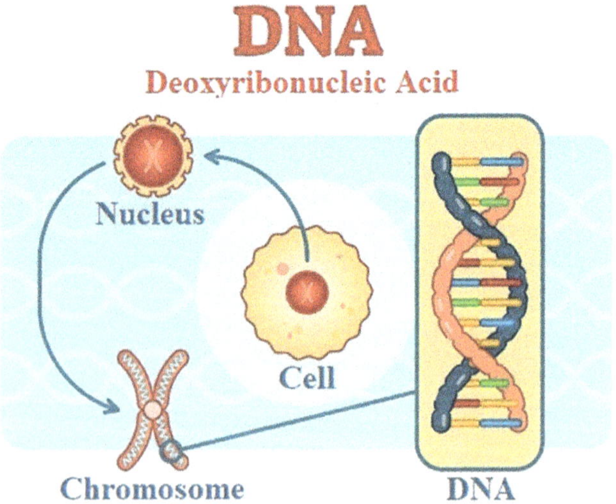

Figure 2

Yes, even one-celled organisms have a DNA code that governs their growth, develops the internal structures, and enables it to carry out all of the life processes. Without exception, DNA is an essential part of the cell division process. The DNA makes a duplicate of itself and the cell divides with each part retaining a copy of the DNA. This is an amazing and complicated process without which no living organism could grow or reproduce.

So out of the "goo," how did this first spontaneous one-celled organism instantly know how to do all these things? If it didn't have DNA, how could it grow or reproduce others like itself? If it did have DNA, who wrote the code? Did you know that the DNA code of a one-celled organism, if unwrapped and written in English, would fill multiple volumes on a library shelf? Is it possible for anything so complex to appear spontaneously from inorganic materials and produce a living organism?

Not only do evolutionists have to answer how the first one-celled organism could carry out the life processes and reproduce, but can they explain how this perfect collection of random, inorganic material in the "goo" came to life? As matter of fact, throughout the world, no scientific research paper has ever been written with evidence to back the claim of the natural origins of life. (ICR)

It is one thing to claim all the material and conditions necessary for life came together millions of years ago, but what force of nature, if not God, gave it life? If this force of nature exists, then following the scientific method in perfect laboratory conditions, scientists should be able to duplicate this process and create life today. But obviously, no such lab experiment exists, or it would be a mandatory part of every high school biology class.

"Intelligent Design" in Bacteria

Since the inception of life on our planet, one-celled bacteria have existed. One feature of bacteria that is quite astonishing to study is a structure called the flagellum. As I mentioned earlier, the flagellum acts like a propeller to move and steer each bacterium through water and mucus. Amazingly, the flagellum is attached to the bacterium by what can only be described as a rotary motor. This rotary motor has many features similar to a common outboard motor used for small boats, but it is microscopic in size, 1/20,000 of an inch. (Strobel, p.856)

Today engineers are always trying to find ways to miniaturize existing technology, so items can be more portable and less expensive to produce. When the size of items are microscopic, the engineering term used is "nanotechnology."

Incredibly, the flagellum beat the world's best engineers by utilizing nanotechnology since the first living organisms appeared on Earth. The following diagram illustrates the complexity of the rotary motor that propels the flagellum. Believe it or not, it even has a clutch that can be engaged and disengaged.

Howard Berg, professor of physics and molecular and cellular biology at Harvard University called it, "the most efficient machine in the universe." Believe it or not, the flagellum can rotate up to 10,000 revolutions per minute and is constructed using 40 different protein parts. (Strobel, p. 852) Is it, therefore, reasonable to believe this complex example of nanotechnology in bacteria happened by chance?

Bacterium "Flagellum" Diagram

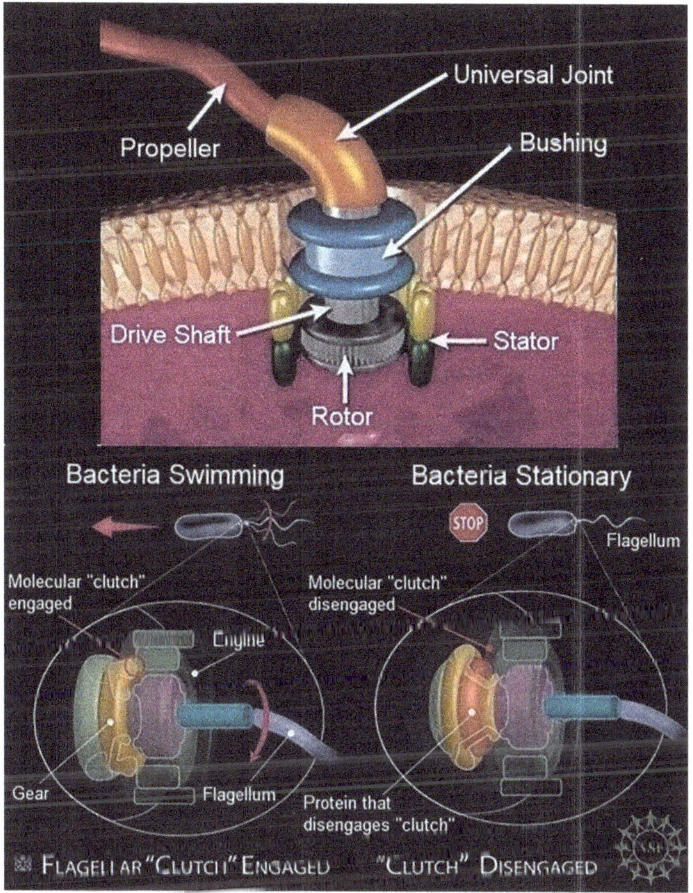

Figure 3

Can "Goo" Lead to Design?

Can evolutionists explain away the "intelligent design" in bacteria that engineers today are just beginning to understand and duplicate? Clearly, mankind has designed various types of motors, but who would have ever thought that the rotary motor was already in use by bacteria long before it was even a thought to a person. Can this evidence of "intelligent design" rationally be explained and duplicated through evolutionary processes?

Evolutionists would argue that over millions of years, advantageous DNA mutations to organisms would occur and be perpetuated due to "natural selection" and "survival of the fittest." Natural processes would eventually lead to designs that were most effective for the given environment, which could include a rotary motor for bacteria.

Evolutionists would also argue that different species of animals demonstrate the ability to "adapt" to their environment like with camouflage. The argument would require that animals with advantageous DNA mutations become the ones that are "selected" by nature to survive and genetically pass on the advantageous features to successive generations.

Ultimately, in evolution, "natural selection" and "survival of the fittest" lead to the weaker of a species having less chance to reproduce and potentially dying off with only the strong remaining. If this process continues over a long enough period of time, then the species will become stronger over time. Eventually, over millions of years, evolutionists believe that advantageous mutations of DNA can lead to more "advanced" design and the formation of new species that are more sophisticated in functionality and cognition than their more primitive ancestors.

"Goo" to the DNA Facts

Since the evolutionist's claim involves the perpetuation of advantageous mutations of DNA, let's look at modern, scientific facts about DNA and its mutations.

First of all, to accept the evolutionist's viewpoint about DNA, you would have to believe that natural processes can create or write the DNA code. You would have to believe that very simplistic DNA originally happened by chance, and over time, natural selection of advantageous mutations continued to enhance the DNA code into greater detail or design.

But research shows that DNA mutations cannot be predicted and typically cause a loss of functionality. Often this diminished capacity lessens the organism's chance of survival. Evolution would require mutations to improve functionality and increase the likelihood of survival, but this is not the case. These mutations have never been found to advance the complexity of a species or enable it to evolve into a new, higher form of species. As matter of fact, increasing numbers of mutations are evidence that DNA only degrades over time.

Every organism is also distinguished by a preset number of chromosomes. For example, the number of chromosomes in human DNA is 46 with 23 from each parent needing to match up with their corresponding pair for fertilization to occur. These differing chromosome counts between species make it impossible for mating to occur outside of a given species.

It is also impossible for a species to add new chromosomes to their DNA code. So primates will always give birth to primates and nothing more. And last but not least, differences in traits within a species are not due to mutations, but are determined by whether the genes passed from each parent are dominant or recessive.

Additionally, in the process of cell replication, the cell's DNA is copied and transferred into the new cell. In the process of reproduction, copies of some of each parent's DNA is passed on to their offspring. So both cell replication and reproduction, over time, involve making copies of copies of copies…of DNA. The fact is that mistakes happen in repeated copying of the DNA just as it does with electronic data that is recopied over and over.

Eventually, copying errors will manifest themselves as disruption in functionality in electronic devices. Either you need to download upgraded software or replace the device. The functionality of life processes in living organisms is also degraded in the form of birth defects, cancer, disease, and other dysfunctions of body processes.

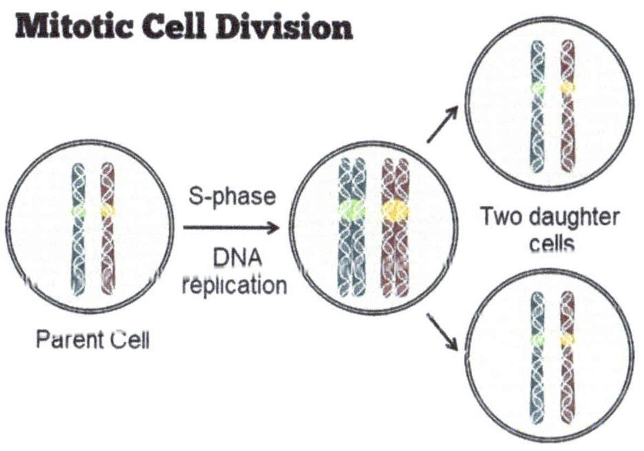

Figure 4

In the human population, geneticists have actually discovered and can trace the "degradation rate" of DNA in the human genome. The fact is that, over time, more and more genetic mistakes are transferred to our offspring. More specifically, human DNA is degrading by about one hundred mutations per new generation. (ICR)

This may be the reason for increasing rates of things like diabetes, attention deficit disorder, and autism. So if humans are the most highly developed organism through evolution, how can evolutionists overcome the fact that our DNA is degrading over time?

In addition, a single human eukaryotic cell contains around three billion chromosomes, and the genetic sequence would fill about 1,200 encyclopedia volumes. (ICR) This is a staggering amount of information and molecular complexity, not just blobs of protoplasm like Charles Darwin believed. So is it reasonable to believe this sophisticated, vast coding system happened by chance through natural processes?

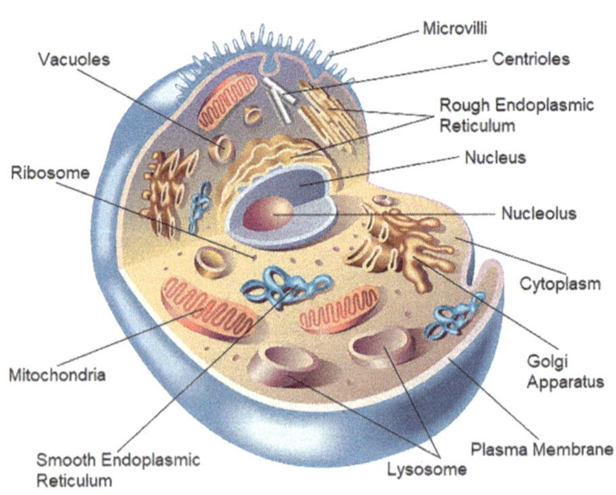

Figure 5

In *The Origin of Species*, Charles Darwin noted subtle differences between different species of turtles and finches in his studies and travels through the Galapagos Islands. For the turtles, he noted differences in in the shell and neck. For the finches, he noted differences in the beak form and function. From these observations, Darwin formulated his Theory of Evolution to explain these adaptations.

How does the creationist explain these adaptive differences within a species? Single-celled and multi-celled organisms do have systems that can sense environmental or internal changes and can react to these changes in a way that benefits them. (ICR) This would include changes in sea turtle shells and differences in the form of finch beaks from one island to the next.

Geneticists have determined that the instructions for these adaptations pre-exist in the DNA code of each organism. Therefore, an adaptation cannot occur that isn't already pre-programmed in the DNA of a given species. So Darwin's observations were correct, but his interpretation was unsound.

How "Goo" Fossils Form?

Since the fossil record is an important part of this debate between creationists and evolutionists, let's look at how fossils are formed. Most people do not realize there is only one possible way for things to fossilize. The plant or animal must be buried completely and suddenly with no access to oxygen, water, or living bacteria.

This sudden enclosure ensures that decay does not begin. The natural process of decay occurs as all things die because exposure to oxygen, water, and/or bacteria will break them down.

Fossils have been found of living animals while they were eating or even giving birth. This can only be explained if these animals were suddenly and violently covered just as they were. Possible sources that could cause this include volcanic activity, mudslides, or major floods. As a rule, well-preserved fossils require rapid burial.

Another important fact about virtually all fossils is that they are found in sedimentary rock deposited by floodwater. A fallacy of evolution often shows animals slowly getting covered by sediment over millions of years, but this is impossible because exposed animals decay or are scavenged. This sediment had to encase them quickly and completely to fossilize them. (ICR)

As a more recent historical example, when Mount Vesuvius violently erupted in AD 79, it covered the city of

Pompeii and its citizens with many feet of volcanic ash and pumice within seconds. Excavations have stunningly revealed people fossilized in place as they were trying to escape the explosion. This tragic event took place about 2000 years ago, yet the people and other organic things have already fossilized. So it doesn't take millions of years to produce fossils. As matter of fact, scientists are now able to produce fossils in the matter of days in the lab. This is another blow to the millions of years evolution requires.

"Goo" Test the Fossil Record

Evolutionists claim in the pre-Cambrian rock layer, the oldest fossils ever found were single-celled organisms. This includes blue-green algae type bacteria and amoeba. Some simple multi-celled plants also appear to have been found, but evolutionists say those were colonies of single-celled organisms that just look like plants. For the sake of argument, let's concede to the evolutionists that every fossil in the pre-Cambrian rock layer was single celled. How can they then explain the Cambrian explosion?

Geologically speaking, with astonishing suddenness, most major animal groups appeared in the fossil record, including those with spinal cords, compound eyes, and articulated limbs. Interestingly, there are no indications of fins turning into legs or feet. Plus, teeth have always been teeth with no non-toothed (proto-teeth) ancestors being found. For the most part, these major animal forms that appeared are the same today with no common origin. (ICR) Today, many scientists believe that "all living phyla may have originated by the end of the explosion," (Strobel, p. 328) which is in line with the Genesis account.

Evolutionists would claim this explosion of new life forms occurred because the climate and atmosphere changed dramatically at that time which enabled evolutionary processes to accelerate. But Darwin himself claimed that evolution requires millions of years of small, subtle changes.

"Charles Darwin"

Figure 6

From Darwin's Own Words

In, *The Origin of Species*, Darwin made the following contradictory statements. According to Darwin, the absence of transitional fossil forms:

"…is the most obvious and gravest objection which can be urged against my theory."

"To the question why we do not find records of these vast primordial periods, I can give no satisfactory answer."

"If it could be demonstrated that any complex organism existed which could not possibly have been formed by numerous, successive, slight modifications, my theory would absolutely break down".

"I concluded that this great group had been suddenly developed at the commencement of the tertiary series. This was a sore trouble to me, adding as I thought one more instance of the abrupt appearance of a great group of species."

"The several difficulties here discussed, namely our not finding in the successive formations infinitely numerous transitional links between the many species which now exist or have existed; the sudden manner in which whole groups of species appear in our European formations; the almost entire absence, as at present known, of fossiliferous formations… are all undoubtedly of the gravest nature."

Can "Goo" Find Transitional Forms?

In the previous quotes, Darwin himself makes a strong case against the fossil record supporting his Theory of Evolution. In particular, he was disturbed by the lack of transitional fossil forms which are necessary evidence of slow change over millions of years. Plus, he couldn't explain the sudden appearance of great groups of species in the Cambrian explosion. Overcoming these points are essential for evolution, but that will never happen.

In addition, every animal species that appears in the fossil record has a unique DNA code that governs its growth and pre-determines its ability to adapt. Knowing that genetic mutations don't improve the functionality of organisms, is it reasonable to believe thousands of new, higher functioning, multi-celled organisms suddenly emerged from one-celled organisms?

Likewise, as Darwin admitted, "Why, if species have descended from other species by insensibly fine gradations, do we not everywhere see innumerable transitional forms?" For instance, dinosaurs suddenly appeared in the fossil record with no chain of transitional forms. Evolutionists claim the giraffe slowly evolved a longer and longer neck over time, but these transitional forms don't exist either. The fact is giraffes have always had long necks.

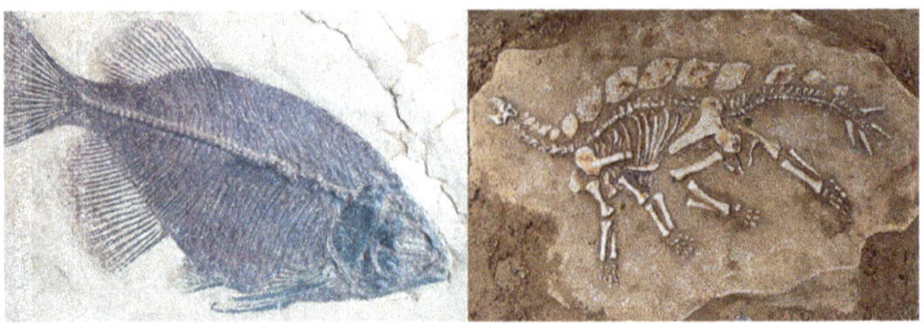

Figure 7

The scientific term to describe how animals stay the same throughout the fossil record is "stasis." Sharks, turtles, bees, jellyfish, sponges, crocodiles, salamanders, zebra, shrimp, flamingos, deer, spiders, ants…are the same today as they appear in the fossil record. Some species have gone extinct, but that has nothing to do with evolution.

A little known fact about fossils is that 95% of them are clams. These are found throughout the world from the lowest of elevations to the highest mountain tops. Interestingly, clams typically open their mouth (shell) when they die, but many of the fossilized clams are closed. So they must have been encased very quickly with sediment. Yet, clams are known to be able to work their way back to the surface when buried in up to five feet of sediment, so the act of burial had to be violent enough to exceed five feet. (ICR)

Even modern evolutionists acknowledge evidence of a catastrophic world-wide flood. Global patterns of continuous sedimentary rock layers have been found on every continent as deposits of this flood. This type of event explains the rapid and deep burial of clams and other animals.

A catastrophic flood, such as Noah's, would also explain the fossils of animals in the process of giving birth and eating. They had to have been overtaken swiftly and violently. A world-wide flood also explains fossils of clams and other marine life on mountaintops.

Darwin's "Evolutionary Tree" Diagram

Figure 8

The diagram above shows the "Evolutionary Tree" which demonstrates the evolutionary chain of animals that Darwin proposed in his theory. Evolutionists contend that through natural selection from advantageous mutations, new species slowly emerged from lower forms of life over millions of years. As you can see, evolutionists believe that our most distant ancestor is an amoeba, and our most recent ancestor is a primate. They also use the "Out of Africa" model to explain the location of human origins. (FYI: Darwin didn't have a degree in biology or any other branch of science. He did, ironically, have a degree in theology. Yet, he is the foundational, authoritative source for evolutionists.)

Creationist "Orchard" Diagram

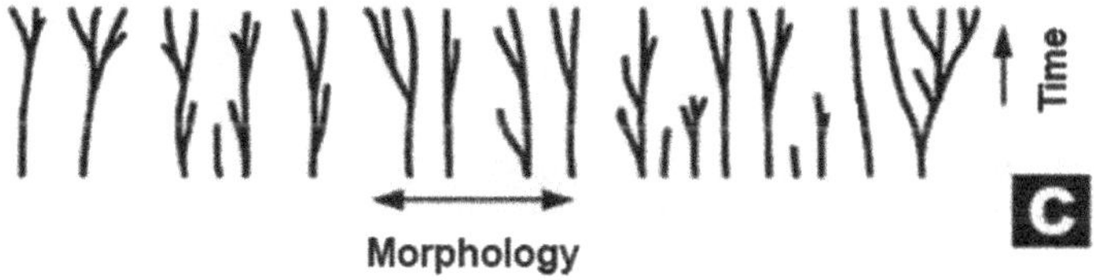

Figure 9

The diagram above shows the "orchard" which is the creationist model to demonstrate how God created animals each
of their own "kind." As you can see, each kind is an independent tree (line), but within some kinds there are branches
of variation. Humans would be an independent tree (kind)
with no branches. The trees with branches would be different
kinds of animals with branches of variation being different
species. Each species would be genetically related with variations within species being determined by pre-programmed,
pre-existing DNA.

Creationists also believe mankind's origins were some-
where in the Mesopotamian River Valley (Garden of Eden)
and continued from the mountains of Ararat through the
descendants of Noah. Modern research of worldwide linguis-
tic and DNA patterns support the spread of all human ancestry coming from this area, not Africa. Powerful evidence lies

in the documented lineage of Noah's descendants. According to the ICR, some examples of traceable ancestries include:

From Ham-Mizraim (Egypt), Phut (West Africa), Cush (Ethiopian "Cushites", South Africa) From Shem-Asshur (Iraq, Iran, Syria "Assyrians", Israel "Semites/Jews") From Japheth-Magog (Russia, Irish, Scots), Ashkenaz (Germany, Anglo-Saxons, Scandinavia), Javan (Java, Japan), Caanan (China "Sinites", known as "Sino"), Tirus (Bulgaria "Thrace")

Amazingly, Magog can also be traced to North American Eskimos, and Phut can be traced to the Olmecs in South America. Likewise, islands established by Tirus on the Aegean Sea, appear to have ties to several Native American tribes. This is strong evidence that we all come from the same lineage, and therefore, the same "blood". What a wonderful revelation.

"Goo" Look at the Structure

Evolutionists would argue that there are many species that are similar in structure and that demonstrates evolution. For example, cats and dogs appear to have evolved into lions and wolves, respectively. That seems logical and has some merit. But on the "evolutionary tree," marine life evolved into amphibians, which evolved into reptiles, which evolved into small mammals and birds. This led to larger mammals, including primates. And last but not least, primates evolved into humans.

Let me first dismantle this argument with an analogy. Assume I asked an architect to design a shed, garage, camp, house, mansion, and skyscraper. For each one, the structure would require a firm level foundation and features including squared off walls, support beams, doors, windows, and protective roofs.

All of these foundational structural features are necessary to construct each of these building types. The final products will be amazingly different, yet they will all share the foundational structural features in their design.

Is it not then logical that the Designer of the universe would also use foundational structural features within each species He creates if that is the best design strategy? So we should not be surprised when we observe similar features between different species of animals. It only makes sense that the same Designer would often use the same foundational structural features.

Likewise, pointing toward cats to lions, dogs to wolves, and primates to humans as evidence of evolution isn't credible for other reasons. First of all, it is an absolute, observable, scientific fact that animals can only reproduce within their own kind or species. No species has ever been observed changing into another species. So cats to lions and primates to humans are impossible.

Since dogs and wolves are in the same species, that is possible, but only because they are genetically compatible. Once again, DNA determines variation within a species, not evolution. So a fish evolving into an amphibian or a reptile is also genetically impossible. The variation, including different breeds of dogs, must come from the existing pre-programmed DNA code.

As another example, primates do share a lot of similar DNA with humans, but there also millions of differences in the code. The similarities are much like the foundational structural features in my building analogy. These shared DNA strands demonstrate that primates share a common Designer or Creator, not that they are our ancestor.

Plus, for a primate to evolve into a human, the millions of differences in the DNA code would all have to simultaneously mutate into extremely higher levels of functioning and cognition. If the mutations happened over millions of years, then there should be evidence of, at the very least, hundreds of "missing links" between primates and humans in the fossil record. These "missing links" are missing because they don't exist. To demonstrate their opposition to the Darwinian Theory of Evolution, more than 1000 scientists and doctors around the world have signed a "Scientific Dissent from Darwinism." (ICR)

"Goo" Should I Date?

One of the big reasons that more and more scientists are dissenting from Darwinism is the huge discrepancy in different radiometric dating systems. To date rocks and fossils, scientists often use elements with a parent / daughter relationship. That means the older one (parent) will eventually decay into the form of the younger one (daughter) over time.

This rate of radiometric decay can be measured, but the problem is that scientists have to guess, and often make false assumptions, on what the starting point should be. This leads to vastly different outcomes depending on the elements used, even for the same rock sample. But more importantly, this leads to the misdating of fossils which are assumed to be the same age as the rock layer they came from, giving a false sense of security to the evolutionist's cause.

For example, ten years after Mount St. Helens erupted, a solidified piece of the newly formed rock was subjected to the potassium / argon radiometric dating system. The system said it was a couple of million years old, but scientists knew it was just ten. In the Hawaiian Islands, a similar test of a rock was done from a recent lava flow. The potassium / argon method gave a date of about 500,000,000 years old. A second test was applied to the same rock using the rubidium / strontium method. This time the scientists came up with 1.5 billion years old. How can this rock that is only a few years old have two tests be so wrong, and worse yet, be about one billion years apart in their results?

In another radiometric dating system, uranium decays into lead. When this uranium / lead system was used to date a piece of zircon, the scientists came up with an age of about one and a half billion years. Unfortunately for the scientists, one of the byproducts of decaying zircon is the release of helium. This rate of release has been scientifically validated, with no assumptions like the others, and it provided a date of about 6000 years old for the same rock. Once again, how can these results be so different?

As a final example, we will look at the radiocarbon dating system, which measures the rate of decay of carbon-14. Carbon-14 exists in all organic matter and has a documented half-life of 5730 years. Radiocarbon dating is accepted as the gold standard by most scientists, but once again, there is bad news for the evolutionists. Carbon-14 is found in measurable amounts in limestone, coal, and even diamonds. According to evolutionists, all of these substances require millions, if not billions, of years to form. But with measurable carbon-14, these substances can only be, at most, a little over ten thousand years old.

The rate of helium release and carbon-14 decay rate are not good news for evolutionists. Evolution requires millions of years of slow, subtle changes, but these two proven radiometric dating systems don't support Darwin's theory.

Just to remind you, the other systems require scientists to pick an assumed starting point of which they cannot prove scientifically. If they believe the results should show millions of years, then they will choose a method with a faulty starting point. As matter of fact, the scientific dating evidence is strongly favoring the creationists who believe in a younger

Earth. Again and again, Science is proving to be a friend to those who promote and defend this young Earth model.

As an interesting side fact, the planet Jupiter radiates energy into the solar system at a measurable rate. That's one reason it is easily seen in the night sky. But at the rate it's losing energy, scientists calculate that it can't be more than about 10,000 years old. Otherwise, it would be an icy, frozen mass of gas by now. Likewise, the measurable energy loss of the Earth's electromagnetic field shows it can't be more than 10,000 years old either. If it was, solar radiation would make the Earth unlivable. Yet another blow to millions of years. (ICR)

Here's one more. Mount St. Helens erupted on May 18, 1980, but what followed a couple years later was astonishing. On March 19, 1982, off the north face, pyroclastic flows and mud flows suddenly and violently carved out a system of hard rock canyons up to 140 feet deep and 17 miles long within a day.

Multilayered sediment deposits were also created which evolutionists would expect to take at least thousands of years. The Toutle River now runs along the bottom of these canyons giving the false appearance that it had been the cause of the erosion. The deepest of these canyons is now called the Little Grand Canyon.

So here's an undeniable, documented example of a natural event that created a canyon system virtually overnight, geologically speaking. Evolutionists believe the Grand Canyon had to have been formed over millions of years of slow erosion by the Colorado River. But the events at Mount St. Helens prove that it could have happened otherwise. In reality, after seeing the formation of this canyon system in such a short time, one would have to argue that something similar to this probably happened with the Grand Canyon too.

Obviously, it would take an extremely violent natural disaster even beyond what was seen at Mount St. Helens. Oh wait, the worldwide geological record shows deposits of a global flood. Yep, that would do it. So the Grand Canyon could easily be much younger than the millions of years evolutionists claim and need to be true. Interestingly, the entire world's fossil record is contained within these multilayered sedimentary deposits.

This is a good point to make something else very clear about the specific rock layers mentioned earlier (Pre-Cambrian, Cambrian, etc...). Each layer is evidence of the order of burial during the worldwide flood. The fossil record demonstrates a logical order of marine life being buried first, then (generally) larger to smaller land animals as flood waters rose. Each new wave of sediment entombed more and more animals as they tried to flee. This all happened in a matter of days, not millions of years, as events at Mount St. Helens modeled on a smaller scale.

Finally, there is another astounding fact that most people haven't heard about. In 2005, Mary Schweitzer, a molecular paleontologist, found something very unexpected after cutting a massive T-rex leg bone. She discovered red blood cells, blood vessels, bone cells, and even hemoglobin and collagen. (ICR)

Typically, paleontologists fully preserve dinosaur fossils and do not cut into them, but this one was so massive, they cut it in half just to move it. This "by chance" cutting of the fossil revealed soft tissue that scientists believed would be impossible to find. Since then, similar findings have being discovered and verified around the world with other dinosaur fossils.

Interestingly, research has found that soft tissues like these will break down and can't exist longer than about 5000 years. So how can these dinosaur fossils supposedly be millions of years old when the scientific evidence is showing them to be thousands of years old? Once again, science is on the side of creationists with this evidence of a much younger Earth.

Can "Goo" Change Your Mind?

Since we already established that DNA degrades over time, is any part of the argument that primates evolved into humans reasonable? One would also have to believe that every genetic mutation within the primate was advantageous and beneficial toward a new species with no defects. This defies modern observation by geneticists who document the negative effects of DNA mutations in humans and monitor the degradation rate.

Unfortunately, this degradation rate also acts like a DNA "clock" leading scientists to predict that humans will slowly become infertile within several thousand years. On the other hand, Earth's current population fits perfectly when calculating out the average human birthrate over four to five thousand years. This is even more scientific evidence of a young Earth. Geneticists do sometimes find mutations that have no notable effect on functionality. But they don't find mutations that perpetuate long term advancement of the organism into a higher order of species.

Evolutionists may then point toward vestigial organs, which are believed to have no apparent purpose, like the appendix, tonsils, and tail bone to demonstrate evolution. But scientists today have proven vestigial organs to be a myth as purpose and functionality have been established for each of these organs. For example, the appendix appears to be used for repopulating the gut with good bacteria that aid in digestion and immunity. (ICR)

The human genome and brain are also impossible to explain, since they're more complex than any computer program ever developed. Our brain is such a monumental leap in function and complexity from a primate's that no evolutionary process can dare explain it. Geneticist Francis S. Collins, head of the Human Genome Project, said DNA was "our own instruction book, previously known only to God." (Strobel, p. 905)

"The Human Genome"

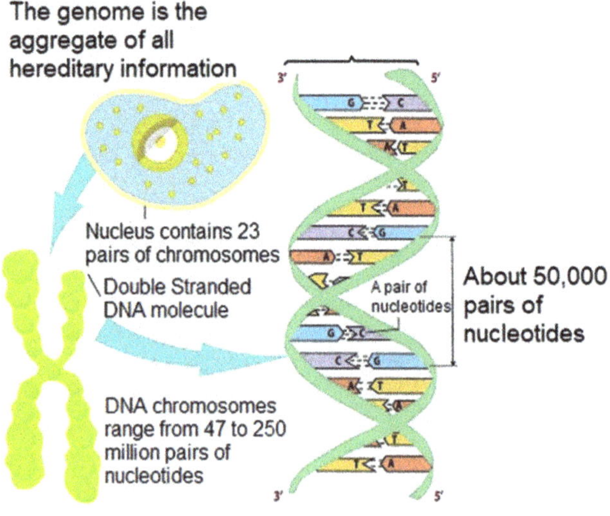

Figure 10

Even Bill Gates, founder of Microsoft, said of the human genome, "Human DNA is far, far more advanced than any software ever created." (ICR) In fact, each one of the thirty thousand genes that are embedded in our twenty-three pairs of chromosomes can yield as many as 20,500 different kinds of proteins. (Strobel, p. 921) So if our greatest researchers and programming minds stand in awe of the human genome, how could it all happen by chance?

On a much simpler scale than humans, think about the metamorphosis of a caterpillar into a butterfly. When compared side by side, the caterpillar and butterfly appear to be completely unrelated, yet they, of course, are the same species. Only due to the genetic engine within the caterpillar is this amazing transformation into a butterfly possible. Evolution could never explain this transformation because it requires millions of years and millions of positive DNA mutations.

Clearly, the miracle of this metamorphosis lies in the pre-programmed DNA code, since this change occurs in only a matter of weeks. Metamorphosis stands as a shining example of what DNA coding can accomplish and evolution cannot. Compared to this complete transformation, adaptations and variations within of species are easily accomplished by DNA.

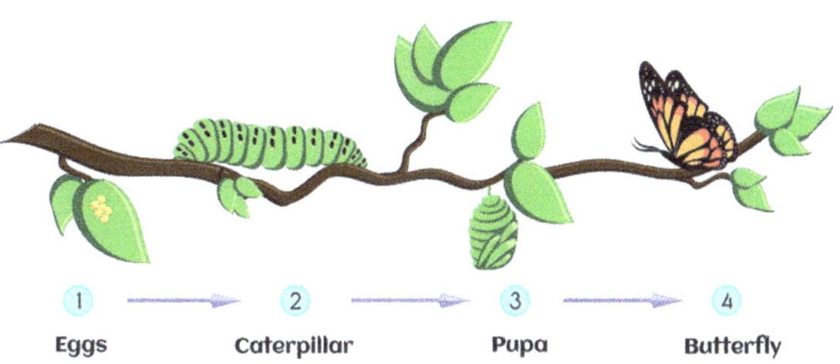

Figure 11

Take a "Goo" Look at the Cosmos

For many years, astronomer Fred Hoyle's belief of a "static," unchanging universe was accepted by most scientists. But another astronomer, Georges Lemaître, believed in a continual state of expansion. In 1919, during a total eclipse, a third astronomer, Edwin Hubbell, proved an expanding universe backed by Einstein's Theory of Relativity.

Scientists around the world came to a consensus that the universe is smaller and denser as one goes back in time. If one goes back far enough, the entire known universe came into being at one point, the "Point of Singularity".

These scientists now believed the origin of all matter, energy, and physical space and time came into being at this point. The universe, therefore, had an absolute beginning from nothing which supports the Genesis account. Today, background cosmic radiation confirms an expanding universe. In addition, most astronomers and cosmologists believe the universe had a beginning, but what—or Who—created the world out of nothing is the question.

Allan Sandage of the Carnegie Observatories said, "We can't understand the universe in any clear way without the supernatural." Robert Jastrow of NASA added, "At a definite moment in time, in a flash of energy and light, the chain of events leading to man commenced suddenly and sharply…"

The Law of Conservation of Matter and Energy states, "Matter is neither created nor destroyed, but conserved."

Since this is a documented, observable truth, only the supernatural can explain creation. How can something come from nothing without supernatural intervention? Moreover, physical law mirrors spiritual law. For example, the combustion engine has transformed our lives and would have worked just as well 500 years ago, but the laws of physics that existed were not fully understood then. Likewise, there is so much we don't understand about spiritual law and the potential it has to transform our lives, but the supernatural has always existed.

As noted earlier, scientists like Sandage and Jastrow believe in a supernatural beginning to our universe. Many scientists also agree with this sudden single point of creation, but they struggle with explaining the cause of this creation. Trying to explain all that exists coming to be through random, natural forces is not possible because it defies the Laws of Physics. Hence, many scientists believe in a Creator through the Kalam Cosmological Argument.

The Kalam Cosmological Argument renders as follows:

Since: 1. Whatever begins to exist has a cause. 2. The universe began to exist.

Therefore: The universe has a cause.

Thus: 1. If the universe has a cause, 2. Then a Creator of the universe exists.

Therefore: Since a Creator of the universe exists, they must be immaterial, timeless, spaceless, and infinitely powerful to create all that is.

The laws of physics and the extreme complexity of galaxies, planetary systems, and living organisms point many toward a "Creator." Some of the greatest minds in history, likewise, came to a realization that the universe has "intelligent design," and therefore, an intelligent designer. Some of these people include Isaac Newton, Louis Pasteur, George Washington Carver, and Werner Von Braun. Amazingly, the two greatest minds of all time, Albert Einstein and Nikola Tesla, also believed in a "Creator."

Figure 12

Creative Signature

Previously, we established the scientific fact that the universe is expanding by studying cosmic background radiation. The rate (speed) of this expansion is called the Cosmological Constant. Earth provides an excellent position (in the galaxy) to detect the cosmic background radiation, which is critically important because it contains invaluable information about the properties of the universe when it was very young. (Strobel, p. 1190)

Hand in hand, this rate of expansion is perfectly coordinated with the force of gravity to form matter. If the rate was fractionally faster, cosmic particles would be too dispersed for matter to form. If the rate was fractionally slower, the matter formed would be too dense, and eventually, gravity would collapse the universe upon itself.

In addition, the nuclear force that bonds the nucleus (control center) of atoms together and the electromagnetic force that bonds particles of opposite charges (+ and -) are perfectly fine-tuned for life. The physical and chemical properties of matter are also determined by these forces, including how they interact to form new substances. The complex molecules and compounds essential for life could not form if either of these forces was fractionally stronger or weaker.

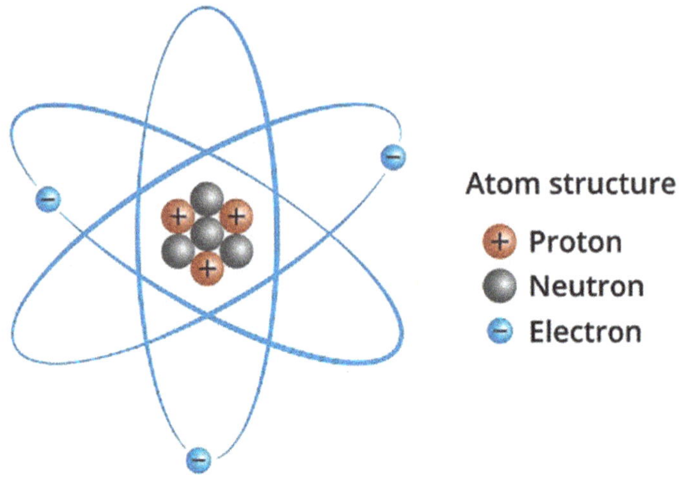

Figure 13

These fundamental forces (gravity, nuclear, and electro-magnetic) of physics demonstrate a delicate balance to sustain complex life. Each is an essential factor that is calibrated to a very specific level necessary for life to exist and for life to perpetuate itself. Scientists have determined that if any of these fundamental forces changed even to a millionth of a degree, complex life could not exist.

In addition, scientists have calculated the odds that all of these essential forces and elements could come together—without a Designer—and create the conditions necessary for life. Astonishingly, the odds are at the very least one in 10^{15}. (Strobel, p. 571) In real numbers that is one in 1,000,000,000,000,000. Wow! That says it all. So is it still reasonable for anyone to think this could all come together by random chance? The "intelligent design," precision of calibration, and predictable relationship between these essential forces is the signature of a "Creator."

Notable Quotes

"*Science without religion is lame. Religion without science is blind.*" *(izquotes.com)*

"*The more I study science, the more I believe in God.*" *(izquotes.com)*

-*Albert Einstein, Physics*

"*Science brings men nearer to God.*" *(izquotes.com)*

"*The more I study nature, the more I stand amazed at the work of the Creator.*" *(izquotes.com)*

-*Louis Pasteur, Medicine*

"*I love to think of nature as an unlimited broadcasting station, through which God speaks to us every hour, if we will only tune in.*" *(izquotes.com)*

-*George Washington Carver*

"The gift of mental power comes from God, Divine Being, and if we concentrate our minds on that truth, we become in tune with this great power." (wisdomtoinspire.com)

-Nikola Tesla, Physics

"For me, the idea of a creation is not conceivable without invoking the necessity of design. One cannot be exposed to the law and order of the universe without concluding that there must be design and purpose behind it all." (izquotes.com)

"My experiences with science led me to God. They challenge science to prove the existence of God. But must we really light a candle to see the sun?" (izquotes.com)

-Werner Von Braun, Rocket Science

"Atheism is so senseless. When I look at the solar system, I see the earth at the right distance from the sun to receive the proper amounts of heat and light. This did not happen by chance." (izquotes.com)

"In the absence of any other proof, the thumb alone would convince me of God's existence." (izquotes.com)

-Isaac Newton, Physics, Mathematics

Our Creator Revealed

It is my greatest hope that by this point every reader is absolutely certain that mankind did not come from "goo." *"I praise you because I am fearfully and wonderfully made; your works are wonderful, I know that full well"* (Psalm 139:14).

Now that we have established there is a "Creator," we must further establish who the Creator is. Many people believe in God, but do they know the one through whom all things were made?

Believing in a Creator is the fundamental first step for non-believers, but there is so much more to know about who our Creator is and what He has done for us. Each of us was created for a purpose and our Creator wants to help us fulfill that purpose through a relationship with Him. And since He is holy, He has provided us the way to set ourselves apart from this fallen world. *"Do not conform to the pattern of this world, but be transformed by the renewing of your mind…"* (Romans 12:2).

Without this relationship with our Creator, we will be caught up with the things of this world and lose forever our eternal purpose and call to a life with Him. Sadly, evolutionists believe they can be here without God, and that steals away their eternal purpose.

For anyone who creates something has the authority to let it fall into disrepair and judge to discard it, or to preserve, renew, and judge to "save" it. The amazing thing about our

Creator is that He allows us to choose to fall into disrepair and be discarded, or to be preserved, renewed, and "saved." The choice is ours to make. We need only to believe on Him and receive His saving grace. The following scriptures show how, in the ultimate act of love, our Creator, the Son of God, became our Savior, the Son of Man.

The Word Became Flesh

"In the beginning was the Word, and the Word was with God, and the Word was God. He was with God in the beginning. Through him all things were made; without him nothing was made that has been made. In him was life, and that life was the light of all mankind" (John 1:1-4).

"The Word became flesh and made his dwelling among us. We have seen his glory, the glory of the one and only Son, who came from the Father, full of grace and truth" (John 1:14).

"The Son is the image of the invisible God, the firstborn over all creation" (Colossians 1:15).

The Humanity of Jesus

"But we do see Jesus, who was made lower than the angels for a little while, now crowned with glory and honor because he suffered death, so that by the grace of God he might taste death for everyone. In bringing many sons and daughters to glory, it was fitting that God, for whom and through whom everything exists, should make the pioneer of their salvation perfect through what he suffered…" (Hebrews 2:9-10).

"…rather, he made himself nothing by taking the very nature of a servant, being made in human likeness. And being

found in appearance as a man, he humbled himself by becoming obedient to death—even death on a cross" (Philippians 2:7-8).

"Since the children have flesh and blood, he too shared in their humanity so that by his death he might break the power of him who holds the power of death, that is, the devil" (Hebrews 2:14).

Jesus Our Lord and Savior

"For if, by the trespass of the one man (Adam), death reigned through that one man, how much more will those who receive God's abundant provision of grace and of the gift of righteousness reign in life through the one man, Jesus Christ" (Romans 5:17).

"But if anybody does sin, we have an advocate with the Father—Jesus Christ..." (1 John 2:1).

"Behold, the Lamb of God, who takes away the sin of the world" (John 1:29).

"He himself bore our sins in his body on the cross, so that we might die to sins and live for righteousness; for by his stripes you have been healed" (1 Peter 2:24).

"God made him who had no sin to be sin for us, so that in him, we might become the righteousness of God in Christ" (2 Corinthians 5:21).

"For I am not ashamed of the gospel, because it is the power of God that brings salvation to everyone who believes" (Romans 1:16).

"For God so loved the world that he gave his only begotten Son, that whoever believes in him shall not perish, but have eternal life. For God did not send his Son into the world to condemn the world, but to save the world through him" (John 3:16-17)**.**

"Salvation is found in no one else, for there is no other name under heaven given to mankind by which we must be saved" (Acts 4:12).

What's the Purpose of It All?

Evolutionist answer:

Through random natural processes, the right temperature, water, inorganic materials, and energy conditions came together to spontaneously create the first living one-celled organism. In an instant, this one-celled organism had all the internal structures to carry out all the life processes, including how to grow and reproduce itself.

Then over millions of years, random, advantageous mutations were passed on through "natural selection" and "survival of the fittest." So by chance these one-celled organisms evolved into new species of multi-celled organisms with more and more complexity and functionality. Ultimately, humans, the highest order of species, happened to evolve through primates, our most recent ancestor.

Creationist answer:

The following scriptures demonstrate the creation of life and granting of dominion to mankind: *"In the beginning God created the heavens and the earth… And God said, "Let the water teem with living creatures, and let birds fly above the earth across the vault of the sky." So God created the great creatures of the sea and every living thing with which the water teems and that moves about in it, according to their kinds, and every winged bird according to its kind… (Genesis 1:1 & 20-21).*

And God said, "Let the land produce living creatures according to their kinds: the livestock, the creatures that move along the ground, and the wild animals, each according to its kind." And it was so (Genesis 1:24).

And God said, "Let us make mankind in our image, in our likeness, so that they may rule over the fish in the sea and the birds in the sky, over the livestock and all the wild animals, and over all the creatures that move along the ground… God blessed them and said to them, "Be fruitful and multiply; fill the earth and subdue it" (Genesis 1:26 & 28).

The following scriptures demonstrate the legal and moral authority provided to guide mankind: *"For the law was given through Moses; but grace and truth came through Jesus Christ" (John 1:17)*. Please notice, Moses was *given* the Law. He was just a messenger. But grace and truth came through the person of Jesus. Please understand, Jesus is grace personified.

"…I would not have known what sin was had it not been for the law" (Romans 7:7). So the purpose of the law was to reveal our sinful nature. No one can fully keep the law and earn their own salvation.

"For the wages of sin is death, but the gift of God is eternal life in Christ Jesus our Lord" (Romans 6:23). Do you see it? By His grace, the purpose of the law was also to show us the need of a redeemer, Jesus. Otherwise, we would inevitably sin and surely die.

"Do not think that I have come to abolish the Law of the Prophets; I have not come to abolish them but to fulfill them" (Matthew 5:17). Please, understand what this means. Christ said he would fulfill them (plural), every Law of the Prophets. If you fulfill your mortgage and car payment, they are paid in full. Therefore, Christ was prophesying His death on the

cross as full payment, in our place, for the consequence of breaking the law. It is finished.

"Know that a person is not justified by the works of the law, but by faith in Jesus Christ" (Galatians 2:16).

"For sin shall no longer be your master, because you are not under the law, but under grace" (Romans 6:14).

"But if you are led by the Spirit, you are not under the law" (Galatians 5:18).

"For I will forgive their wickedness and will remember their sins no more" (Hebrews 8:12).

Summary: With the best of intentions, no person can keep the literal or moral intent of the law. Failing to keep the law is inevitable, so we must set our hopes on God's atoning grace. For those who don't know or believe on Jesus's finished work at the cross, disappointment, guilt, and condemnation are certain to prevail. On the other hand, in Christ and His purpose of salvation, there is no condemnation. *"The Lord himself goes before you and will be with you; he will never leave you nor forsake you. Do not be afraid; do not be discouraged"* *(Deuteronomy 31:8).* No amount of self-condemnation can supersede Christ's sacrifice.

For whoever believes in Him will have *"eternal life, and they shall never perish"* (John 10:28). As God's children, your sin debt has been paid in full, so just believe and receive. Remember, *"Abram believed the Lord, and he credited it to him as righteousness"* (Genesis 15:6). Please understand, righteousness doesn't mean you're perfectly holy. It means you have right standing with God because of your faith. Becoming sanctified (holy) is an ongoing process from your right standing. So let yourself live under his free supply of grace, and stop trying to meet the demands of the law. You are uniquely and divinely created, so stop trying to impress those of this world. Let His grace be your root, then holiness will be your fruit. Be uncommon.

For Christ's life as the Son of God is infinite. Therefore, his atoning death at the cross is infinite in time, scope, and number. So even as we will surely fall, His blood will continue to cleanse and restore us.

Figure 14

Weighing the Answers

Evolutionists:

Let's go back to the observations of Darwin from the 18th century. He contemplated variations he saw within species of finches and turtles and developed a theory to explain these variations. Darwin expanded his theory to include the natural origins of life and how it evolved over time.

No scientific research has ever observed the evolution of living creatures into different species or spontaneous generation of life coming from non-living, inorganic materials. Since the precepts of evolution have never been scientifically observed, tested, and repeated using the scientific method, evolution should not be presented as fact, but only as unproven theory.

Creationists:

Let's go back to the observations of Einstein and Tesla from the 20th century. As they pondered the laws of physics that give order to and govern the universe, they concluded there is a Creator and there was a specific moment of creation. Today, most scientists, including evolutionists, agree in this moment of creation and can't dispute the fact that life only comes from life, biogenesis.

"Great are the works of the Lord; they are pondered by all who delight in them" (Psalm 111:2).

"For we are God's handiwork, created in Christ Jesus to do good works, which God prepared in advance for us to do" (Ephesians 2:10).

"By faith we understand that the universe was formed at God's command, so that what is seen was not made out of what was visible" (Hebrews 11:3).

"The heavens declare the glory of God; the skies proclaim the work of his hands" (Psalm 19:1).

"The sea is his, for he made it, and his hands formed the dry land" (Psalm 95:5).

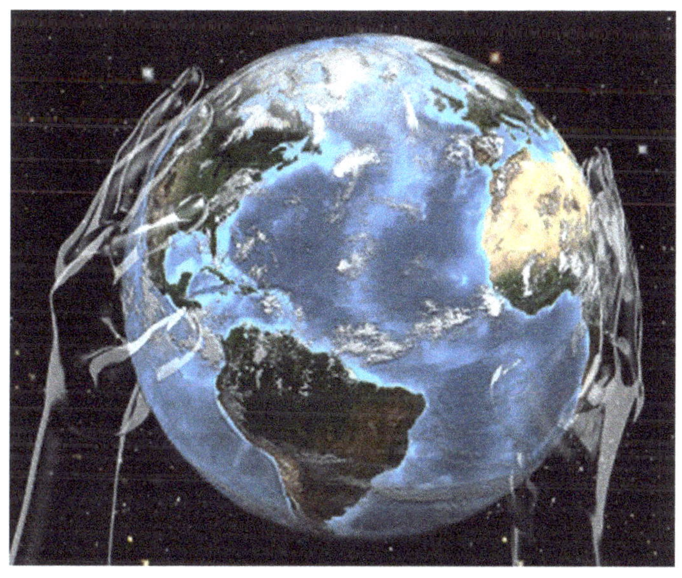

Figure 15

The Final Choice

I hope this book has given believers a set of tools to enhance their public profession of faith. More importantly, I pray that the facts in this book act as seeds to bring as many non-believers to Christ as possible so they can know and receive his grace.

Redemption and healing are Christ's free gift to humanity by his shed blood and broken body at the cross. In an extreme act of love, Jesus took our place and bore our punishment. By doing so, he defeated the sting of death and sat at the Father's right hand because his work of salvation for us was finished. The sacrifice of Christ is once and for all for past, present, and future sins. Remember, it is about what Christ did for you, not what you can earn or deserve. For there is no condemnation in Christ Jesus. The only thing you must do is believe on his shed blood and accept his free gift of grace. For faith is the currency of Heaven.

"Not by works, so that no one can boast" (Ephesians 2:9).

"I am the way and the truth and the life. No one comes to the Father except through me" (John 14:6).

"Come to me, all you who are weary and heavy laden, and I will give you rest" (Matthew 11:28).

"My grace is sufficient for you, for my power is made perfect in weakness" (2 Corinthians 12:9).

"For I am convinced that neither death nor life, neither angels nor demons, neither the present nor the future, nor any

powers, neither height nor depth, nor anything else in all creation, will be able to separate us from the love of God that is in Christ Jesus our Lord" (Romans 8:38-39).

As a child of God, your choice is to have a loving relationship with the Word (our Creator), who became flesh (Jesus), and redeemed us by his shed blood at the cross (finished work for "sin debt" and "healing"). Or you can choose the religion of evolution by believing in a random, spontaneous, chance creation from "goo." I pray you choose, the Lord our God, because…

Figure 16

Fact Review "Cheat" Sheets

- Spontaneous generation to "life" of inorganic material has never been observed
- Stanley Miller (1953), and others, have only created simplistic, non-living amino acids
- Biogenesis (life only comes from life) is an observable, documentable scientific fact
- No scientific research paper has ever produced evidence of the natural origins of life
- DNA in one-celled organisms can fill multiple volumes of library books (By chance?)
- DNA governs the growth and reproduction of one-celled organisms (Who wrote it?)
- If not God, what force brought the first one-celled organism to life? (Is it repeatable?)
- The intelligent design of the flagellum demonstrates nanotechnology (10,000 rpm)
- DNA does not become more complex or gain additional code over time (Geneticists)
- Ability to adapt pre-exists in DNA, not by natural selection or survival of the fittest
- Fossils had to be violently and completely encased not to decay or be scavenged
- A catastrophic flood explains "marine" fossils on mountaintops worldwide

- Global patterns of sedimentary rock layers are evidence of Noah's worldwide flood
- Most major animal groups suddenly appeared in the Cambrian Explosion
- Cambrian Explosion fossils demonstrate "stasis" (No transitional forms.)
- Darwin's "evolutionary tree" shows our ancestors range from amoeba to primates
- Darwin didn't have a degree in Biology or any branch of science (Not authoritative.)
- Darwin's quotes about lacking fossil evidence disprove his own theory of evolution
- Within 2,000 years (not millions), people were fossilized by volcanic ash at Pompeii
- Most radiometric dating systems are inaccurate for samples of known younger ages
- Carbon-14 is in measurable amounts in coal and diamonds (half-life of 5730 years)
- Canyons up to 140 feet deep and 17 miles long formed within a day (Mt. St. Helens)
- Multilayered sediment deposits were created too (not 1000's of years) (Mt. St. Helens)
- Energy loss rate of Jupiter/Earth's electromagnetic field show at most 10,000 years old
- Multiple soft tissue discoveries in dinosaur fossils can't be more than 5,000 years old
- "A Scientific Dissent from Darwinism" is signed by over 1,000 scientists and doctors
- No scientist has ever observed an organism evolving into a new species
- No "missing links" exist between primates and humans (Should be at least hundreds)

- Biblical ancestry and world linguistic/DNA patterns disprove "Out of Africa" origins
- Human DNA has a measurable "degradation rate", so humans are not evolving
- Evolution requires millions of years of millions of positive mutations, not degradation
- Human birthrates support Earth's current population originating 4000/5000 years ago
- Discovered functions of vestigial organs has disproved an evolutionary cause
- "Human DNA is far, far more advanced than any software ever created" (Bill Gates)
- Matter is neither created nor destroyed, but conserved requires a supernatural creation
- Einstein, Tesla, and other scientists believed "intelligent design" requires a Creator
- Nuclear and electromagnetic forces are perfectly calibrated for complex life to exist
- The fundamental forces of Physics are God's "Creative Signature"

Bibliography

Institute for Creation Research, (ICR), https://www.icr.org/homepage/

Creation in the 21st Century, https://www.tbn.org/programs/creation-21st-century-david-rives / ICR

VCY America, Christian Information Radio, *Science, Scripture, and Salvation* program/ ICR

Strobel, Lee. The Case for a Creator Student Edition (Case for... Series) Zondervan/Youth Specialties. Kindle Edition.

http://www.wisdomtoinspire.com/a/NJ64j85s/15-of-nikola-teslas-most-intriguing-quotes

https://izquotes.com/author/albert-einstein;https://izquotes.com/author/louis-pasteur

https://izquotes.com/author/george-washington carver; https://izquotes.com/author/wernher-von-braun/

https://izquotes.com/author/isaac-newton

Figure 1: Amoeba—ID 34406447 & Euglena—ID 34424805 © Designua | Dreamstime.com

Figure 2: DNA—ID 108044162 © VectorMine | Dreamstime.com

Figure 3: Flagellum Motor (top)—Image from "A Question of Origins", eternal-productions.org/ Anne Loria

Figure 3: Flagellar "Clutch" (bottom)—Credit: Zina Deretsky, National Science Foundation

Figure 4: Mitotic Cell Division -ID 41929459 © Zainebs | Dreamstime.com

Figure 5: Human Cell—ID 27673358 © Rob3000 | Dreamstime.com

Figure 6: Darwin—ID 101420216 © Boldurevaol | Dreamstime.com

Figure 7: Fish—ID 122080627 © Marlon Brathwaite | Dinosaur—ID 118303526 © Maksim Shchur | Dreamstime.com

Figure 8: Evolution—http://www.rtgmin.org/2012/06/08/evolution-theory-of-evolution/ answersingenesis.org/ Steven Wright

Figure 9: Orchard—https://i0.wp.com/www.rtgmin.org/wp-content/uploads/2012/06/creation-orchard1.jpg/ answersingenesis.org/ Steven Wright

Figure 10: Human Genome—ID 112651440 © Vitalii Zhurakovskyi | Dreamstime.com

Figure 11: Metamorphosis—ID 130916747 © Inkoly | Dreamstime.com

Figure 12: Einstein—ID 84998950 © Janusz Pieńkowski | Tesla—ID 140093094 © Zenobillis | Dreamstime.com

Figure 13: Atom—ID 137799817 © Fenix84 | Dreamstime.com

Figure 14: Crucifixion—ID 122993034 © Biblebox | Dreamstime.com

Figure 15: Hands Holding Earth—ID 3132802 © Michael Brown | Dreamstime.com

Figure 16: Cross—ID 137732498 © Nirmala Dsouza | Dreamstime.com

About the Author

I am a lifelong educator of 28 years from the great Upper Peninsula of Michigan. I have held many different jobs and titles over the years, but my current job description is the most unique. Since my K-8 school only has six students, I wear the hats of teacher, administrator, and last but not least, bus driver. And yes, I said six students. This is an amazing little school where the kids get all the attention they need, maybe more than they would like, and everyone feels like part of a big family. I truly love my job.

On a more serious note, I am a survivor of stage four non-Hodgkin's lymphoma which was throughout all of my bone marrow and in every lymph node. I was diagnosed in December of 2013 and started the first of 18 sessions of chemotherapy in January of 2014. Eventually, I was cancer free for about 2 ½ years until lumps appeared on my cheek and forehead. After a month of radiation in August of 2018, I am cancer free and ready to get on with my life.

This humbling time in my life made me reflect more deeply on my faith as I began reading the Bible and studying about the grace of God more earnestly. Recently, I've had a couple of vivid dreams about things I would say to defend my faith to a non-believer. As a teacher, the scientific facts in this book came to me as essential to make a compelling argument. Plus, the title "From Goo to God" kept rattling around in my head. So I stopped making excuses and just thinking about things and decided to write it all down.

This is the first book I've ever written, and I can honestly say, I was compelled to write it. Every time I would see evolution present as fact, it would turn my stomach. And even worse, when people of faith are ridiculed because they believe in a Creator, it makes my blood boil. So I'm just at a point that I can't look the other way when I see the religion of evolution being forced on our kids and society. If you feel the same way, please join me in this fight.

My health scare also made me realize that none of us knows what tomorrow will bring, so we have to take advantage when opportunity knocks. I need to know that I've done everything in my power to ensure my family and friends belong to Christ. This book gives me the opportunity to have that conversation that may not have occurred otherwise. It's worth the risk. Plus, I hope I can help strengthen the faith of fellow believers, and more importantly, plant a seed of faith in the heart of those willing to listen. For as the Father lovingly declared, "This is my Son, whom I love; with him I am well pleased. Listen to him." (Matthew 17:5). Because faith comes from hearing and hearing by the Word of Christ.

www.ingramcontent.com/pod-product-compliance
Lightning Source LLC
Chambersburg PA
CBHW050015040726
47599CB00014B/1386